Don't Settle for Less

Don't Settle for Less

Gaining a Full Recovery from Your Accident

GLENN HONDA

EXPERT PRESS

Don't Settle for Less
Gaining a Full Recovery from Your Accident

ISBN-13: 978-1-946203-49-6
ISBN-10: 1-946203-49-1

This publication is designed to provide accurate and authoritative information regarding the subject matter contained within. It should be understood that the author and publisher are not engaged in rendering legal, accounting or other financial service through this medium. The author and publisher shall not be liable for your misuse of this material and shall have neither liability nor responsibility to anyone with respect to any loss or damage caused, or alleged to be caused, directly or indirectly by the information contained in this book. The author and/or publisher do not guarantee that anyone following these strategies, suggestions, tips, ideas or techniques will become successful. If legal advice or other expert assistance is required, the services of a competent professional should be sought.

Recovery Law Center
1260 Young Street, Suite 228
Honolulu, HI 96814
808-597-8886
www.recoverylawcenterhawaii.com

Expert Press
www.ExpertPress.net

Contents

Introduction	1
Chapter 1: My Mother Made Me Do It	3
Chapter 2: My Principles of Practice	9
Chapter 3: Auto Accident Stories	15
Chapter 4: Motorcycle Accident Stories	27
Chapter 5: Premises Liability: Susan's Story	33
Chapter 6: Justice for Tina	37
Chapter 7: Serving Clients in Many Ways	43
In Conclusion	49
About the Author	53

Introduction

WHY DID I CHOOSE to write this book? I have been a practicing attorney for 25 years, 20 of those years with my own firm. My focus has always been personal injury law, and I've been in this business long enough to have a lot of stories to tell.

My goal here is not to present Personal Injury Law 101, but rather to share some of those human stories. These are stories of folks who have suffered damage or injury, generally through no fault of their own. It has been my privilege to help them deal with a system that is often stacked against them.

One of my hobbies is photography—I spent a year after college studying photography in England—and I think the photographer's eye for detail informs my approach to every case. I take the time to look not only at the big picture but also the underlying details. That approach has served me and my clients well through the years.

While I have the experience and know-how to be a big-box law firm, I choose to remain a small firm. Why? We are here to help injured people find justice. For me, that means taking the time to really listen to each individual's story.

Allow me to share a few of those stories with you in this book. These are all real-life cases from my practice; names and details have been changed to protect the clients' privacy.

Let me start by telling you a bit of my own story.

Chapter 1

My Mother Made Me Do It

THE TITLE OF THIS CHAPTER probably sounds like a joke. It's not.

I was born and raised here in Hawai'i. And from the time I was very young, my mother—my very own "tiger mom"—ingrained in me the notion that I would be either a doctor or a lawyer. Why? She was convinced that doctors and lawyers were the most successful people. I actually wanted to be a pilot. It turns out that pilots make more than lawyers. Who knew?

Of course, years later, my mother denies up and down that she ever insisted on any such thing. But I remember being asked when I was a little boy what I wanted to be when I grew up. The words would just come out of my mouth automatically: "A doctor or a lawyer." There was never any other answer; it never even occurred to me that there could be any other answer.

After high school, I went off to college at Creighton University in Omaha, Nebraska. That might seem an odd choice for a kid from Hawai'i, but I really loved it there.

In Hawai'i, there were a lot of people who went into the military after World War II. The GI Bill allowed veterans to get scholarships to various colleges, and Creighton was one of the universities that offered those scholarships to GIs. Because of that, a lot of professionals from Hawai'i ended up going to Creighton and the school developed a really strong reputation here in Hawai'i.

For me, it turned out to be a really great school. It's a little bigger now, but when I went, there were only 3,600 undergraduates, and there is something really wonderful about going to a small school. It's a community. The small classes and the individual attention made for a great learning environment. I loved it.

I thought I would do the doctor thing, but it turned out that I hated science. I love hearing about it, but I hated learning about it. I also discovered that I didn't do well with blood and disease—to this day I have to force myself to look at people's injuries—and I'm something of a hypochondriac. If I were to see a patient, and they started telling me their symptoms, I'd convince myself I too had whatever was wrong with them. So there was just no way I could be a doctor.

By the time I had done that first semester with the sciences, I knew medicine was not going to be for me. I considered going into psychology—after all, psychologists are doctors, right?—but that didn't seem right for me either.

I decided it was time to try my mom's other option, so I took an internship with the Judge Advocate General in the Air Force. I was in court—obviously not appearing, but helping the lawyers with their cases—and I loved it. I switched to the law school track and when the time came, I did really well on the LSAT. I could have gone to other places, but I really loved Creighton, so I went to law school there.

After I finished my degree and before I headed to law school, I got to go study abroad for a year. I went to Kensington College in London, where I studied photography and became really engrossed in the life in London. I had such a wonderful time there that I was reluctant to leave.

In fact, I wanted to stay in London so badly that I changed the reservations for my flight home from Pan Am to British Airways, just so I could hold onto a bit of England for a little while longer.

When I finally landed in Honolulu, I had three or four calls from folks wanting to make sure I was okay, and I had no idea why. Then I learned the horrific news that the Pan Am flight had been blown up over Lockerbie. It turned out that my desire to keep that connection to England just might have saved my life.

I returned to Creighton to attend law school. To be honest, my mother was not the only one who encouraged me to become a lawyer. When the time came, my grandfather paid for most of my law school tuition. My family is Japanese, and my grandfather was interned in a camp during World War II. He received reparations money from the government, and gave me a portion of that money to pay for my legal education. He told me he wanted me to "become somebody and fight for justice."

As I was approaching my law school graduation, I learned that my dad had been diagnosed with colon cancer. When I came home to see him, the doctor pulled me aside and advised me, as the oldest son, to start getting our affairs together because my dad had perhaps only a few months left. I hadn't intended to move back to Hawai'i, but with that news I decided to come home after law school graduation and live here for a while to be with the family.

We tried to get everything together, and we spent a lot of time just doing family stuff. I was able to develop a much closer relationship with my dad, and we're still very close today. Fortunately, he beat the odds and survived that dire diagnosis. Ironically, he actually outlived his oncologist. I'm just grateful that we now have such a great relationship.

After settling in Hawai'i, I never really thought again about living somewhere else. I had always imagined myself living in LA, or San Francisco, or Seattle—living in some bigger city and working at a big, glamorous law firm. But that wasn't to be. Now I can't imagine living anywhere but here. I really like the culture, and the food, and friends and family being around. Now I really have no interest in living anywhere else.

I returned to Hawai'i after law school and got my law license in October 1993. Finding that first job as an attorney was a challenge. Jobs were scarce. It seemed no one was hiring, not even the government. I had a few interviews, but nothing panned out. I started pounding the pavement—literally—going door to door with my resume and writing samples.

Cold calling law firms didn't get me any job offers, but it did get me a lot of good feedback and encouragement. I remember one lawyer coming out from the back office and saying, "I don't have anything, but I just want to commend you on your guts to go around making cold calls to law firms. If I had anything, I'd interview you in a minute."

I was looking really hard for a job, and a lot of people knew I had been looking really hard for a job. A friend of my mom told me about a law firm in Kailua, on the other side of the island. He said they were doing pretty well and were looking for an associate. They had already interviewed a lot of people, so I didn't have high hopes, but I figured I could at least use the opportunity to practice my interviewing skills.

We're pretty casual here in Hawai'i—you seldom see lawyers in neckties unless you're in court—but I went down to Kailua in my necktie and jacket. As I sat there in the waiting room, I was so self-conscious; it was as if I could just feel all the eyes of all the secretaries staring at me. Eventually I was summoned into the senior partner's office for the interview. I thought it went really well, but as I was leaving, one of the secretaries said, "Oh, you're done already?" That seemed like a bad sign, since a short interview usually means you're out of the running.

So I left there and headed back to downtown Honolulu, about 40 minutes away. I was discouraged and decided to go work out. Much to my surprise, in the middle of my workout, I heard my name paged over the intercom for a phone call.

It turned out that the law firm was trying to find me, and my tiger mom had struck again. No one had cell phones then, of course, and poor, unemployed, brand new attorneys like me didn't have beepers either. The law firm found my mom's friend, who found my mom, who tracked me down to the gym. That's where I got my first job offer: on the phone at the gym, standing there in my shorts and t-shirt. They asked if I could start on Monday and I did.

It wasn't exactly a dream job at first. It seemed to me there was a lot of hazing and some were trying to set me up for failure. I wasn't getting good stuff to work on, and I was actually looking for things to do. I was even running copies and doing things like making calls for medical records. And it wasn't exactly a lucrative position; I was making $6,000 a year less than my secretary.

It was frustrating at the time, but the upside was that I learned how to do all of these basic tasks in my sleep. I can quickly evaluate a claim or go through mountains of medical records. Then they started letting me format demands, and to this day, I can write a settlement demand letter from memory. I don't need the form; I can just type it out. All the parts of the form just flow right from my fingers.

Things changed when the other associate, who had been giving me a hard time, went out on leave for a while. The senior partner asked me to do some work for him. I must have impressed him, because from that point I was given more and more responsibility directly from the boss. I never had to do work for that associate again. As I began to feel more an integral part of the firm, I came to really love what I was doing.

Once I hit my stride, I really did well. I started meeting a lot of medical providers who were sending me business, and I developed the biggest portfolio of all the firm's associates. That really drew the attention of the partners. I was doing really well and I loved it.

Eventually the senior partner approached me about becoming a partner at a new firm he was starting. I loved my job, but I had hit the glass ceiling there, so I agreed to join him.

Unfortunately he had to abandon our plans because of a personal tragedy, so I decided to make the leap myself and go out on my own. Even though I was working out of my bedroom for the first couple of months, I was doing really well. I still had my referrals coming in, and the clients in my portfolio chose to come with me. Within a couple of months, I had made more money than I had in the entire previous year as an associate with the old firm.

Once I had enough money to buy a desk and set myself up in an office, I did that and haven't looked back since.

My first secretary didn't even know how to type when she started with me, but she was very loyal. She was a little older than I am, and she was married to an attorney. When I started my practice, I was still in my late 20s, and her being older seemed to give me a bit more credibility. Her Filipino background and language ability helped a lot with our Filipino clients.

She was with me for 20 years, and retired just recently. She stayed with me through many changes, through a large expansion and then a contraction of my practice. Now I'm the sole attorney, and I have a staff of two paralegals, a legal secretary, a clerical person, and a bookkeeper.

We're a small firm, and I prefer it that way because it allows me to give each of our clients the personal attention they deserve. As a smaller firm, we can get to know our clients better. Working so closely with them, we do develop personal relationships, and over the years we have made some good friends. That's one of the most rewarding parts of this work.

Chapter 2

My Principles of Practice

AS I LOOK BACK, I realize that over my 25 years of practicing personal injury law I have developed some personal principles for the way I practice.

What I have always wanted to do as a lawyer is to help people solve problems. When I graduated from law school I thought I would be practicing some kind of corporate law. But when I landed my first job, it was with a firm that focused on personal injury law. As I immersed myself in the field, I came to love it and now I can't imagine myself doing anything else.

Of course there would be satisfaction in helping people or businesses with something like a will, or a trust, or a contract—the kinds of things I expected to be doing as a corporate lawyer—but I've come to realize this work helps people in really profound ways. We're able to level the playing field for our clients and fight for justice the way my grandfather wanted me to do.

I get great satisfaction out of helping people recover compensation for the injuries that they have sustained, especially when they're not getting anywhere on their own. They're often getting the run around from insurance adjusters or from insurance company attorneys, and when we step in we put a stop to all that nonsense. The shenanigans end when we become involved, because the other side knows that we know what we're doing, and if they were to fight us, it would be very expensive.

It would be nice to be able to say that everyone involved in a case is always open and above reproach, but unfortunately that's just not true. I've seen cases where defendants lied. I've seen cases where adjusters lied. But they know lying to us can be very risky. Just the defense knowing that there's an attorney on the file gives the client a better chance at a fair recovery. It's gratifying to know that the final outcome for the client is usually better than it would be if they tried to work through the case on their own.

What's different about our practice?

I actually hired a senior adjuster from an insurance company to come work with me as a paralegal. She and I had been on opposite sides for more than 20 years, but we had a good record of being able to settle our cases, and she liked the way I practice. So let me tell you a little about that.

We try to keep a friendly, welcoming atmosphere in our office and I think that encourages clients to feel comfortable sharing their stories with us. We do take a personal interest in people. My paralegals, George and Jolie, are so personable that even new clients feel like they're our friends already.

What sets us apart? I don't want to say we're bleeding hearts, but I suppose sometimes we are. My best friend in the law is on the other side. She's a defense attorney, and she's always called me a sap. I'll say, "I want to help people. His life has been ruined. He needs more compensation than that." Her response is always, "You're such a sap."

Maybe I am. Maybe we can actually sometimes be a little sappy. That's because we want to make sure that we can do the best job we can for our clients. That doesn't always mean getting more money. We look at the big picture. It might be possible to secure more money from a trial down the road, but that can be a long, painful, and stressful process. It can be two years or more of uncertainty—spending tens of thousands of dollars on experts and trial preparation—and even if the award is greater at the end, the client may not end up receiving more money. There is real trauma involved in going all the way to trial. People don't truly realize that until they're in the middle of it.

Although personal injury attorneys work on a contingent fee basis, meaning that the client doesn't pay out any money up front, attorney fees and expenses do come out of any eventual settlement or award. So if you are the client, sometimes your best result is settling for a little bit less than you would like, because it takes less time and can be more cost effective. Because the costs will be less, you wouldn't have to give up as much of your settlement as you probably would after a trial. And you would not have to go through two and a half years of depositions, examinations, and the agony of waiting to learn whether you are going to win or lose. All of that goes away if you settle. We don't always recommend settlement, but sometimes settlement is a better outcome, and we want the best outcome for our clients.

I think that the fairest settlements are those where the plaintiff takes a little bit less than he or she wants and the defendant pays a little bit more than he or she wants. If anybody walks away fully gratified from a settlement, somebody's giving up too much or taking too much.

Some firms want to settle quickly and easily. They run the risk of leaving money on the table. Other firms are so determined to maximize the dollar amount that they go all out—maybe from hubris—and fight unnecessarily. I think that is a two-fold disservice to the client. On the one hand they try to settle as quickly as possible to meet their bottom line; then on the other hand they may have an exaggerated opinion of their skills, and thus risk their client getting nothing.

We take a different approach. We focus on achieving the best overall outcome for the client, whether by settlement or litigation. We consider how long it will take to get the client their just compensation, what it will take to do that, and what the risks might be.

I believe that settlement is an art. Sometimes the art is persuading clients that this is actually in their best interest. I had that difficult conversation with a client just recently. I was recommending that he accept a settlement offer, and I noted that an arbitrator had already ruled against him. He was indignant. He told me that if he was in the wrong, he wanted to be told that by 12 jurors. I knew that if he went to trial and lost, he would likely end up paying some of the other side's attorney fees and costs. I had to talk him down into a more modest, realistic settlement.

In the end he finally realized that I was doing the best I could for him, keeping his interest in mind. Once he understood this, he was grateful that I had been able to talk some sense into him. He decided against taking the risk of not only losing any compensation, but also having to pay the other side. He was pretty grateful and I was happy with how the case ended. I won't make money from that case, but that's the nature of personal injury work. Working on contingency is always a risk.

The contingency fee is typically a third of the settlement or verdict. I understand completely that a third sounds like a lot, but that's because of the risk we take as personal injury attorneys. The client doesn't pay up front and doesn't pay by the hour. It can be years before the attorney is paid. A one-third fee has become the standard because of the risk.

How we decide to take a case

In considering any case, we do like to get involved right away; ideally there is communication with the insurance company. We never ask you to wait, or call us back when you reach tort-eligible status.

When we evaluate the case, we don't just look at it in terms of monetary value. We often find ourselves working for clients who have been turned down by other firms. Larger firms may do only a cursory evaluation; if a case doesn't meet their predetermined criteria—if they can't check all the boxes on their list—they'll often decline the case. We don't use a checklist. We're going to sit down with the client and take the time to talk with them. We'll pull out our toy cars and our paper and pencil to have them show us how things happened. We're going to look at every different angle that we can use to help them.

Obviously, we're not able to take every case. This is a business and it's how we support ourselves. But we believe in meeting genuineness with genuineness. When someone comes to us, and they're not getting any help from anyone, and we believe they're sincere, it motivates us to look even deeper to see if there's something the other firms have missed. More often than not, we're able to find a way to help the client.

Even if they've been rejected by another firm, we want to hear them out. We'll have them come in and we'll dig deeper into their story. Maybe they're just not really good at explaining. So explaining is something we would do for them. So we'll have them show us with the cars and paper and pencil. If they seem sincere and genuine, and we're able to piece together an honest story that we're comfortable with—one that we think that we can work with—then we take the case.

I think we give people more of a chance to tell their story than some others might. I believe in giving them the benefit of the doubt. My staff jokes that "If you can't get Glenn Honda to believe you, then no one will believe you."

So I should point out again that we don't actually accept every case that is brought to us. Not every prospective client proves to be credible. Just as an example, let me tell you about the most memorable case that I didn't take.

It was not long after I started my own practice. I had just hired my first associate, Melissa. She was just out of law school, very smart and capable; she spoke three languages.

It might even have been her first week on the job. She wanted to see an intake. In a normal intake, the potential client comes in and we hear their story. We decide whether or not to take the case; they decide whether or not they want to hire us.

So Melissa was sitting in with me on this lady's intake. It seemed perfectly normal at first. We joked a bit, trying to make each other comfortable, and then I started going through the simple intake procedure.

We hadn't even gotten to her accident yet. I was just gathering basic information. When I asked if she had any children under the age of 18, a very serious look came over her face, and she said, "Oh, yes, I've had thousands of kids." I thought that she meant it figuratively, that she was maybe a church lady or social worker or a coach—someone who had worked with thousands of kids over the years and considered them all her kids.

But the look on her face was so serious that I probed a little further. And she said, "Yes. Every time they come to get me, they seed me with at least a thousand children, and I give birth to them all." She went on a little bit more explaining about her alien abductions.

I didn't want to seem insincere or dismissive, but I could barely contain my laughter. So I got up and said, "You'll have to excuse me for a minute."

I went outside, closed the door, and got the giggles out of my system. When I went back inside, she was still talking, and poor Melissa was just sitting there, wide-eyed, listening intently.

She didn't know what to do. We listened to this woman for another hour before we finally got to the accident, which turned out to be just ridiculous. She was hit by a shopping cart, and she claimed that the store employee had actually propelled the cart toward her on purpose. Of course in those days we didn't have cameras everywhere, so there was no visual evidence. And anyway, she was hardly believable.

So we ended up not taking that case, but we gave her a couple of hours because I wanted to let her have her say. When the woman finally left, Melissa was too shocked to have found it amusing. It wasn't until the next day that she was able to see the humor. It became a running joke in our office for the five years that Melissa worked with me. Interviewing the alien mother together must have been a bonding experience; we're still good friends. She practices law in Australia now.

Chapter 3

Auto Accident Stories

SINCE AUTO ACCIDENTS are by far the most common cases that we personal injury lawyers see, you'd think it would be easy to find an attorney to help you after you've been in an accident. Unfortunately, it doesn't always work that way.

Some firms actively avoid auto accident cases that don't fit into their ideal model. These "non-ideal" cases are ones in which:

- The accident is not a simple rear-ender.
- The case is not tort-eligible, meaning that the claimant hasn't yet incurred $5,000 in medical costs.
- The injuries don't appear substantial.

When you call these firms, you can tell that the paralegal, or whoever initially screens the call, is checking the boxes, making sure you fit the perfect model. If you don't fit the model, meaning it wasn't a rear end accident with clear liability, and there were no broken bones or substantial injuries, then they're just not interested. They will turn you away.

We hear all the time from clients who have been turned down by other firms. When they've called enough of these places, they begin to feel that their case is just not worth anyone's while. They may even get so discouraged that they don't hire an attorney at all.

The unfortunate truth is sometimes clients are not able to adequately describe how the accident happened, especially if they've never been in an accident before. In Hawai'i, we have a lot of immigrants who don't speak the language perfectly, and so have difficulty describing what happened, but they're not the only ones. Sometimes even native speakers cannot convey how the accident happened in a way that will persuade someone that there is liability. If you're on the phone just checking boxes, you're not going to be looking into that case as carefully or deeply as we will. You're going to turn that case away because you don't see liability.

As I said in the previous chapter, we are always willing to listen, and we are willing to take smaller cases. We believe that everybody has a right to a claim, and smaller claims are okay with us. People with smaller claims deserve good legal representation too. So we do take smaller cases.

If we can't understand right away how the accident happened, we'll look at the case a little longer and a little deeper than most of the "box checkers" will. And when we do that, sometimes we'll see that the case is not as small as it was thought to be. It can turn out to be bigger than everyone thought it was, including the client and the other firms.

It's important to remember that a case that seems small to the lawyers is still a big thing for the client. Each person's case is very personal to them. If you are the injured party, you may think your case is huge. Part of our job is to look as deeply and as thoroughly into your case as possible, and then to tell you objectively and honestly what we think. Sometimes what we have to say is not always what the client wants to hear.

We like to take cases as soon as possible. If you've been in an accident, insurance companies will be trying to call you and get statements from you. They'll record what you're saying, and they will provide you with information that may or may not be accurate. So unlike some other firms that want you to wait until you've reached tort eligibility, we prefer that you call us right away.

Why? There are a lot of mistakes that can be made before your case is tort-eligible. Our way of doing business is to have you to come in earlier so that we can help you avoid the mistakes, pitfalls, and misinformation that could harm your case later. If you wait to come to us after you have reached tort threshold, there may be some mistakes that are not fixable, or that will take a lot more work to fix on the back end then they would have on the front end.

I believe it's worthwhile to spend a little more time with a client, do more work in the beginning, and then monitor their case while they get treatment and work towards tort eligibility. From the client's perspective, they are likely to have a lot of questions, especially in the beginning of the process. With us they not only have a law firm that is very experienced in these auto claims, they also know they can call us anytime to get their questions answered. As our client, you can call us anytime, and find out what the truth is, instead of relying on what your friend said, or what your uncle heard, or what the insurance adjuster may be saying.

Sometimes what you think the insurance adjuster is saying is not what they're really saying. Sometimes it's a misunderstanding, but sometimes—and I hate to say this, but it's true—they're just outright lying and giving misinformation.

Here's an example right from my own experience. My aunt was once involved in an accident. Fortunately her injuries weren't severe. She did have some muscle kinks and stiffness, though, and she wanted to get some massage treatment to deal with that

So she called to report the accident and to find out the specifics for her coverage. She said, "I'm not really going to make a claim; I just want to get some massages to work out the stiffness." The call was on speakerphone, and the insurance adjuster on the other side said, "Oh, your policy doesn't have massage therapy, so I'm sorry but we wouldn't cover that. You would have to pay for that on your own."

That was a blatant lie. Every single insurance policy in the state of Hawai'i covers massage therapy that is prescribed by a doctor. There is no insurance policy in Hawai'i that would not cover massage therapy. That's how I know that there are lies.

When clients come to me and they said, "Oh, the adjuster said this, this, and this," it's true that sometimes you've misunderstood the adjuster, but other times, as I have personally experienced, the adjuster lies.

Let's look at a couple of actual auto accident cases that illustrate the way these cases proceed.

Margaret's story

Margaret's accident happened when she was making a left turn across an intersection. In many cases, the driver turning left is at fault for causing the accident, but in this case Margaret was turning on a left green arrow.

There was a car in front of her and another behind her, all turning left on the green arrow. The defendants, a married couple, were approaching from the opposite direction, and for some reason, either mistook what they saw, or weren't paying attention, and also started to cross the intersection. Of course, when there is a green arrow the opposing traffic always has a red light, without exception.

These defendants claimed that Margaret was the cause of the accident. Eventually they said that she was not crossing on the green arrow.

The intersection was three or four car lengths wide where the impact occurred. The defendants had three lanes to cross over, and plenty of time to see these cars crossing in front of them. The defendants' claim that they didn't see Margaret crossing right in front of them meant they simply were not paying attention, no matter what color the lights were.

The defendants' story kept changing. First they said Margaret was crossing on the red light and shouldn't have been crossing. Then they said the collision was "just a rub," despite the fact that the bumpers came off and the husband wasn't able to open his side door where the collision occurred. It clearly wasn't a rub; no rubbing impact makes your bumper fall off. The husband even admitted that he was in the intersection picking up parts of his car and he was angry.

The couple's stories evolved from the original recorded statement they gave to their insurance company, to the version of events that they gave to their attorney, which was provided to us in the discovery process, then to the versions they gave in their separate depositions. Their story changed yet again at the time of the arbitration hearing, and we took full advantage of that.

Margaret had insisted that it was the wife who was driving that night, and that they had switched places. So when I deposed the husband I asked him if he had been driving, and he said yes.

I asked him why he was driving, and he said he was the main driver of the car. I also asked him why the car was not in his name. Was it his wife's car, since it was in her name? He said, no, it was his car and they just didn't put the proper name on it.

The truth was that he was not able to insure a car because he had a couple of DUIs on his record. His license had been revoked. I asked him about the DUIs and he confirmed them. He was not supposed to be driving and he knew it. His license had been revoked about two years earlier.

So I said, "Does your wife know that your license has been revoked?" He said, "Yes." I said, "You're sure she knows about the DUI and the license revocation?" He said, "Yes, because she was there sitting in court with me." These people told so many lies and their story kept evolving.

When I deposed the wife, I told her that my client said she had been driving, and I asked her if there any reason that her husband would or should not have been driving. She said, "Oh, there's no reason. He drives at least half of the time. There's no special reason he was driving that night."

They even accused Margaret of faking her injuries. They said she looked fine when she got out of the car and then as soon as the police showed up she started grabbing her neck and pulled out a cane to walk with. They claimed she was walking around with a cane for sympathy.

The truth of the matter is that she had never needed a cane before. She didn't have it at the time of the accident; she got the cane from the hospital where she was treated after the accident. This particular lie came out at the arbitration hearing, where Margaret was carrying the cane that had been dispensed to her from the hospital. It even had the name of the hospital on a label, along with her name and the date of her hospitalization.

Throughout the entire process, the defendants' lies just kept increasing. At first the husband said that he was not driving, but that he was looking up from the passenger seat and saw that the light was green for them and red for Margaret.

I said to him, "Are you sure there was no cars turning in front of my client on the left turn?" At first he said he wasn't sure because he was looking at his phone. So I said, "If you were looking at your phone, how did you see the red light in front of you?" He stumbled over that, but then said he saw the red light when the car moved forward.

His wife, on the other hand, said there was a car in front of Margaret, but that Margaret was following so closely behind the other car that the wife couldn't see it. That was simply absurd. There's no way that a left-turning car blocks the sight of the next car turning left behind it.

It was lies after lies after lies, and I just brought all of that out at the hearing. It was really easy to cross-examine these people and destroy their credibility, and so of course we won the case.

The outcome was especially gratifying because this one accident had made such a lasting impact in Margaret's life. She was in her late 50s at the time and prior to the accident, she was pretty active physically. She was a teacher by profession, but her main passion was hula and teaching hula. She used to go to various events where she would dance hula and do the Hawaiian prayer with hula.

After the accident she gained quite a bit of weight because she couldn't move freely anymore. She had suffered some low back injuries and nerve damage that made it hard for her to walk without help from the cane or a walker. It was hard for her to stand. She used to like to go searching for Hawaiian herbs in the forest, but after the accident, she could no longer do that because the terrain is too uneven for somebody to walk with a nerve injury.

Margaret gave up an awful lot because of her injuries. She's in her 60s now, and she's heavier, so she's had to make lifestyle changes.

Even with that, she's going to have some kind of impairment for the rest of her life.

Margaret was a nice lady, perhaps a little naïve. When we told her that the defendant was saying that it was her fault she was just flabbergasted. She couldn't believe that anyone would have the audacity to lie under oath about an accident being their fault. Of course, doing what I do I knew it happened all the time, but she was just shocked.

In our first meeting with her, she was so sincere. We felt that she was telling the truth, so we decided to take the case even though the liability was disputed and it was a left turn case. It wasn't until I started getting into the ever-evolving stories of the defendants that I realized we'd be able to win pretty easily.

Margaret was a classic example of a client who came to us having been rejected by other law firms. She really did need to make a claim, but she kept getting rejected because it was a left turn accident. That's a disqualifying box for call screeners.

Another factor was the way she was describing what had happened. She said she was turning on what she called a protected green light. I don't think anybody else took the time to clarify what she was saying, so they didn't understand what she meant by the protected green light. If the box checkers had taken the time to learn that it was not just a green light but a green arrow, they might have taken her case a little more seriously.

Janet's story

Janet was a transplant from the mainland who had been living in Hawai'i for some time. Her accident happened about ten years ago. Unlike Margaret's case, Janet's case checked all the boxes. On paper, it was a model case. One, it was a rear-end collision; two, the damage was pretty bad; and three, she was hurt and she went to the emergency room.

So Janet didn't have any trouble getting a big law firm to take her case. She started treatment for her injuries, but as time went by, the firm was getting reports from the doctors, and it didn't seem like she was progressing very quickly. She herself didn't feel that she was making very much progress, or that the treatment was helping her. She was going fairly regularly for treatment, but not as much as the other firm would've liked, because she wasn't reaching the tort threshold quickly enough. They may have feared she wouldn't reach the threshold at all.

So at some point Janet's law firm made a decision—I can't say how or why, since I was not privy to their thinking—and they called her in for a meeting. So she drove downtown, 20 or 30 minutes from her home, to go and meet with her lawyer.

She went up the elevator, and as soon as the elevator doors opened, there stood one of the paralegals from the firm. Janet stepped off the elevator and the doors closed behind her. Then the paralegal proceeded to tell her, "I'm sorry, we're not going to take your case anymore. We're not representing you anymore. Here is your file, and here are some cards of some other lawyers that may take your call and look at your case."

And then the paralegal pressed the down button, guided Janet back to the elevator, pressed the lobby button, and let the doors close. Janet just stood there stunned. She didn't know what to say. She didn't know what to ask or anything. She was just in shock. She said that by the time the elevator reached the bottom floor, she was in tears. And even as she told me this story, she was in tears.

Mine was not one of the cards they gave her. She said she knew she couldn't possibly go to anyone that that firm recommended. She just threw those cards away, and asked some friends, and my name came up.

She didn't know what to do. She was so happy that we would even take a look at her case, and that I as the attorney would come out personally to meet her. With that other firm, she never did meet with any of the attorneys, only a paralegal. And it wasn't even the same paralegal who met her at the elevator that day.

We met with her, and I decided there was nothing wrong with the case, so I took it. It turned out that one of Janet's vertebrae was fractured in the accident. I'm pretty sure the other law firm didn't expect that.

Before we make a claim for you, of course we wait until you are tort-eligible, but we always like to say we want you to be sufficiently better that we know the full extent of your injuries.

Until you are 60 to 80 percent better, we really don't know what your claim is going to be. And in this case, the other firm didn't wait that long. Janet wasn't even 30 percent better when they dismissed her as a client.

When she did finally reach the 60-ish percent level, and it had taken her so long to get to that point, the doctors decided it was a bit strange, so they did an MRI and found the vertebral fracture. She also had some nerve damage and needed back surgery.

In the end, we were able to settle Janet's case fairly and prudently, since there was clear liability on the part of the other driver. If the other firm had just had the patience to stay with Janet throughout her recovery, they would have found it to be much more valuable than they originally thought.

Rob's Story

Rob was stopped in a left turn lane waiting for the left arrow when he was hit. The young woman who hit him was in her mid-20s, but she only had a learner's permit at the time; her father was in the car with her as the required licensed driver.

The father admitted that they were merging to the left lane, but he claimed that Ron was trying to overtake them, which made no sense, because to overtake them, he would have had to cross over into a busy lane of oncoming traffic.

They admitted that before the collision, they didn't see Rob behind them, to the side of them, or in front of them. The front end of their car hit the rear end of Rob's car, so he could not have been overtaking. The driver and her father both had a bad credibility issue. Neither of them remembered seeing Rob at all, so there was no way they could definitively say how the accident happened. They couldn't remember anything. They had no proof or explanation as to why they thought that Rob was moving and trying to overtake them in oncoming traffic. They just were not willing to admit the simple fact that this inexperienced, unlicensed driver had made an improper left merge.

We took Rob's case and filed a lawsuit for him. His situation is complicated by the fact that his health is precarious. Sometimes he's okay; sometimes he's not. He is only in his 50s but he has lung cancer from working on the railroad. He had to go on disability, and moved to Hawai'i for the warmer weather. The case took a lot longer than we expected, and there were times we thought he might not make it to the end of his case.

The biggest delay was caused by the defendants ducking the process server. They moved residences three times—for "personal reasons," so we were told at their deposition. They would hide inside the house when the process server came, and they would ask their friends to lie for them. It was quite difficult to serve them. We even had to get the insurance adjuster involved. We told him that we were trying to serve their defendant and if they kept evading service we would tack that onto our damage claim.

The adjuster knew we meant business, so he also tried to get them to accept service, but they still wouldn't comply. They wouldn't return his phone calls. I used one of my online searching tools to find them, but I couldn't get any more information because they kept moving. Eventually I was able to find a relative, the father's brother.

I called the brother and explained that there was no reason for them to evade service because he was fully insured. I told him that the insurance company was going to get him an attorney, pay for the legal fees, and pay for any settlement or award. There was no need for them to hide. Eventually the brother called the defendants and we were able to serve them, but it took over a year to get service on them.

In the end we prevailed because the defendants' story was so inconsistent. I was certain they were lying. At the deposition, I asked the daughter—the driver—if she had any independent recollection of Rob trying to overtake them. I was pretty sure that she didn't, and she kept avoiding the answer. I finally asked her "yes or no"—if she saw him trying to overtake her, because that was what they were alleging—and she started to cry. In my mind, that meant that she was lying and she at least had some remorse about it. I figured the father was calling the shots. I think that's why she cracked under pressure: maybe she didn't want to lie but her dad was urging her to do so. We'll never really know. I could have brought that up to the arbitrator, but there were enough holes in their story that nobody bought it, and that was how we won.

The common thread in these cases—Margaret's, Janet's, and Rob's—was our taking the time to dig deeper into each one. I'm proud to be able to say that we were able to produce a good outcome for each of these good folks.

Chapter 4

Motorcycle Accident Stories

PEOPLE WHO GET INTO ACCIDENTS while they're riding a motorcycle often find themselves at a disadvantage when they seek to pursue a claim. Beyond the misfortune and injuries of the accident itself, they often face prejudice from insurance adjusters and attorneys, as well as jurors and arbitrators.

Many people see motorcycling as reckless behavior, and unfairly consider it part of a reckless lifestyle. When they see someone who fits their image of a biker—maybe with tattoos and piercings—they immediately assume that person was at fault in any accident. I sometimes see that same bias against riders of bicycles or mopeds, but it is most common with motorcyclists.

So given that inherent prejudice, you will not be surprised that we often see motorcyclists who come to us after having been turned down by other firms. Like the auto accidents I described in the last chapter, these are cases that don't easily fit into the mold of a perfect case. Motorcyclists sometimes can't even get an appointment with a law firm. And yet, the injuries in these accidents are usually severe. The victims need and deserve representation; their accidents need to be investigated thoroughly.

Ryan's story

When Ryan had his motorcycle accident, he assumed that he would be able to use the big law firm that had represented him in a previous accident. He had been seriously injured as a pedestrian when he was hit by a pickup truck. He was in the hospital and rehab for weeks, and when the case was finally resolved, that big law firm made a six-figure fee from that case.

When Ryan tried to call his previous lawyers, he couldn't even get one of them on the phone. Ryan was badly injured in his motorcycle accident. They didn't return his calls, and when he finally did reach them, he was rudely told—by a paralegal, not even one of his lawyers—that they would not take the case.

Ryan and his family were completely distraught. They were so angry. They felt the lawyers had acted like his best friends when he had a big case for them, and yet wouldn't hear him out on this second case. They wouldn't even give him an appointment.

The family tried calling some firms that specialize in motorcycle accidents but no one really would really listen to the whole story.

When Ryan called us, we were the only ones willing to give him an appointment. To be honest, the case didn't seem very promising at first, based on what the defendant was saying—they were disputing liability—and even the way Ryan was describing what had happened was a bit difficult to picture. We went back and forth a few times by email and telephone, and then we finally met with him.

He came in and he seemed very sincere, but even as we listened to the story in person, it still sounded that the accident could have been his fault. He wasn't describing it very well, so it became one of those times where we actually had to pull out a piece of paper, have him draw the accident scene, and use our toy cars to show us what happened. It was then that we finally knew he had a case.

The accident happened on the freeway. We have a zipper lane for high occupancy vehicles (HOV) and motorcycles to use. Access to the HOV lane is via an onramp, a diagonal lane that goes from the regular freeway traffic lanes to the HOV lane. There is a movable barrier that is used to change the direction of the lane, because part of the time it is an HOV lane and part of the time it is an oncoming traffic lane.

Ryan was in the onramp to the HOV lane when he was hit. He claimed that the defendant swerved into the onramp at the last minute, causing Ryan to get hit and fall to the ground. He suffered some pretty serious injuries. He was wearing protective clothing, so he didn't get much road rash, but he did have leg and arm fractures and was laid up from work for several months.

The defendant in the case claimed that Ryan was overtaking him and was not actually in the onramp lane. I was concerned that the defendant seemed so adamant about his version of events, but both of my paralegals advocated strongly for Ryan, so we took his case. He really did seem honest and sincere.

Initially it seemed that both versions of the story were somewhat plausible. But as the case proceeded, Ryan proved to be the more credible witness.

When I took the defendant's deposition, he continued to insist that Ryan had been overtaking him and was not actually in the onramp lane yet. So I asked him, "When was the first time you saw my client?" He replied that he only saw my client after the collision. That response begged the question: Then how could he know that Ryan was trying to overtake him, and how could he know that Ryan wasn't already in the lane like he said? Of course he had no explanation for that.

I asked if he turned his head to look into the lane he was trying to merge into. He said no, but he did look in the mirrors, and didn't see anything. He might have been describing a blind spot, but the driver is still required to turn his head and look. The defendant had no explanation for why he hadn't seen Ryan.

The defendant's story turned out to be really flimsy. There was no way he could be so certain that Ryan was overtaking him and still claim that he never saw him prior to the collision. He could not say with certainty that Ryan wasn't already in the onramp. I thought he made a very bad witness. His response to almost everything I asked was, "I don't know."

Ryan, on the other hand, was a much stronger witness. He was consistent in his story and very believable.

Despite all that, we didn't want to leave things up to chance so we continued to look for other witnesses. We got a lucky break while we were talking to the investigating police officer on a different case. He told us that there was a witness but they hadn't gotten a statement. The officer still had the witness's name in his notes and he put it into the police report.

With the help of some online research, we finally managed to track down the witness. He was difficult to reach—it took us weeks of leaving messages—but we were finally able to find him. Once we met him, we learned that he hadn't been avoiding us; he just had an unusual work schedule.

He remembered the accident, though, and told us exactly the same thing Ryan had. He said he saw Ryan in the onramp and the defendant swerving into the lane at the last minute.

So we took his deposition and he seemed very credible. It was shortly after his deposition that the defense counsel caved and settled the case.

We were able to get a really good result for Ryan, and I believe that result came directly from our willingness to go the extra mile and dig a little deeper into the case. I think that's what sets us apart from other firms.

Jeff's story

Jeff's case is a challenging one, and is still awaiting resolution as I write this book. The accident happened late at night. He was on his motorcycle approaching an intersection on a curve. The defendant, driving a large SUV, was making a wide right turn from the intersection into the curving road where the accident happened.

There were several big factors weighing against Jeff in this case, and those made it difficult for him to find representation. First of all, there was the simple fact that it was a motorcycle accident, so there was that built-in prejudice against motorcyclists. Second, although he was seriously injured in the accident and had the presence of mind to safely navigate the approximately 39-minute, 11-mile trip from Waikiki to Aiea, when he was taken to the hospital his blood testing indicated that he may have been over the legal limit for blood alcohol. In Hawai'i that's not a deal breaker, but it doesn't help when you are looking at liability. He was not arrested for DUI.

Because Jeff was badly hurt and taken to the hospital right away, the police report is somewhat one-sided on the defendant's story. So a lot of attorneys just did not even give him the time of day.

It was a horrific accident. Jeff's injuries were really severe. The first thing he remembered when he was coming back to consciousness was the doctor asking him how many testicles he had because they only saw one. When he said he had two, the doctor actually had to reach in and pull the other one out of the body cavity, which of course was enormously painful. His next memory was screaming in pain before again losing consciousness.

Afterward, he was laid up for three or four months at home. He lives in a two-story house and because his leg and pelvis were broken, he couldn't go up the stairs. So he had to camp out downstairs. His wife had to take care of him, and she was expecting a baby any day. When the baby was born, he was not able to help take care of her. It was just an awful situation for them.

Jeff came to us about a year and a half after the accident. The insurance company had already denied liability. On meeting him, we found him to be very credible, authentic, and sincere. Even though he had been drinking on the night of the accident, he seemed very clear about how it happened. He could even recall hearing his motorcycle brakes making certain sounds, just before the impact. So we looked at all the pictures, listened to what he had to say, and decided to take his case.

After we took the case, we started investigating the defendant and discovered that he had a terrible driving record. He had two prior DUIs and had lost his license twice. He even lost his license for a third DUI a few days after our accident. He also had a history of getting into fights, even one with a police officer. He was a pretty unsavory character.

I got an accident reconstructionist to come out and look at the accident scene. He said that, based on his calculations, the defendant had to have been making a wide turn, crossing into the oncoming traffic lane, and was just coming back into his own lane when the collision occurred. That's important because this was late at night. When he made that wide turn, at some point he was in Jeff's lane of travel, meaning that his headlights were pointing in Jeff's face.

What the accident reconstructionist believes—and the physical evidence bears this out—is that Jeff saw the headlights coming, tried to get out of the way, veered left, and that's when the collision occurred. He was trying to escape what appeared to be oncoming headlights in his lane. The defendant was correcting back into his own lane of travel, so they were both correcting in the same direction. We believe that if the defendant had made a proper right turn, he would have always been in his own lane and the accident would never have happened.

Of course when we deposed the defendant, he couldn't really remember anything. He had a selective, yet otherwise vague memory of how he believed—or wanted to believe—how the accident happened, but when I questioned him about his past driving record he said he couldn't remember. He couldn't even remember which lane Jeff was in just before the accident.

There was a lot about his story that didn't add up. At the accident scene, he actually reversed his vehicle. He gave two different reasons for that. First he said that it was because he couldn't find the motorcyclist and so he wanted to be out of the way. That made no sense, because if he didn't know where Jeff was, he risked hitting him again. Then he said that the motorcycle caught on fire and he didn't want his truck to be too close. What I think is that he wanted to make very sure that his truck was firmly in his own lane when the police arrived.

As I said, this case is still awaiting resolution, but I am hopeful that we will reach a good outcome for Jeff.

I do think both of these cases illustrate just how complicated a motorcycle case can be, and how the system can work against victims in these cases.

Chapter 5

Premises Liability: Susan's Story

A PREMISES LIABILITY CASE is a specific type of personal injury case, in which a property owner is held responsible for an injury that happens as a result of some unsafe condition on their property. These cases, often referred to as "slip and fall" or "trip and fall" cases, and carry their own set of challenges. These cases can be really difficult to pursue. Jurors in these cases tend to look at a plaintiff and say, why weren't you paying attention? Why weren't you looking? There is a common prejudice against these plaintiffs, an assumption that somehow, the plaintiff could have prevented the incident. Juries often say that they should have been looking and been more careful.

Here's the truth of the matter: When we're going about our business, most of us are just looking ahead. If you're in a store, you're shopping. You're not looking for water on the floor. You're looking for the items you intend to buy. That's the truth, but people don't always take that into consideration. Maybe it becomes armchair quarterbacking, assuming the victim should have been more careful. But that's very common in premises liability cases.

Largely because of this tendency to blame the victim, some liability is usually attributed to the plaintiff in a premises liability case. Let's take a look at how things played out in a premises liability case I handled a few years ago.

There are also other types of premises liability cases, for example, Susan, a nurse in her early 50s, suffered a serious back injury when a heavy gate fell on her. It was a driveway gate, one of those heavy gates—about 500 pounds—that roll back and forth to allow cars to enter or leave a residential property.

When the accident happened, Susan was on foot, walking around the gate, which was slightly open. She didn't touch the gate, but as she walked around it, the gate suddenly fell over and pushed her to the ground. She was briefly knocked out by the impact.

Apparently the gate was not installed properly, which is why it was able to fall. Susan lived on the property and knew that this gate had fallen previously, so as discussed earlier, a jury might well have determined that she had some liability in this incident, reasoning that she should have been more careful.

When Susan came to us, she had already been working with another attorney, but was not satisfied with how the case was going. I am always wary when a client approaches us because they are unhappy with their existing representation—you have to be concerned that they might turn on you too—but after hearing her out, we thought we could help her. We decided to take the case.

I called the other attorney and told him we were taking the case. He considered her something of a difficult client, so he just wanted out. In fact, unbeknownst to us, the attorney had actually filed a motion to withdraw, had a hearing, and had the judge let him out of the case. He was serious about this.

When we took over the case, a lawsuit had already been filed, but there had been a lot of delays. We found things in the court file that needed to be fixed, and we took care of that.

In the meantime, Susan's health took a turn for the worse. Her back was so sore that at times she was bedridden. She went to three different doctors. Orthopedic doctors turned her down saying she was not a surgical candidate but she really thought there was something wrong with her. She finally consulted a neurosurgeon, and the neurosurgeon said that although she did not have positive electro diagnostic findings, he felt that her symptoms were consistent with herniation of the disk.

The doctor decided to operate, found that there was actually a herniated disk, and fixed it surgically. She had very good results from the surgery, though she did have to have a second operation because of some leaking from the disk. The neurosurgeon said that type of leaking after the fact happens in about 20 percent of these cases.

The defense, representing the landlord of the property, tried to argue that she didn't really need the surgery. They claimed that she was shopping for a doctor, having seen three orthopedists, all of whom turned her away. Of those three, two have a reputation for being "cutters." The defense argument was that if those doctors did not consider her a surgical candidate, then she did not really need the surgery.

What made the difference here was that this particular neurosurgeon was probably the most respected in town. When asked why the orthopedists turned Susan down, he explained that neurosurgeons and orthopedists have different standards. He said from his experience, this was without question a surgical case. While he humbly and diplomatically tried not to cut down the orthopedic surgeons, he said he disagreed with them and so he recommended surgery for Susan.

Later, after the case, the defendant's counsel admitted to me that our neurosurgeon would have been nearly impossible to discredit not just because of his reputation, but his knowledge and expertise came across clearly in his very articulate testimony.

In the end, we were able to resolve Susan's case in an arbitration hearing, and produced a good result for her, almost a $300,000 award. It was a very good outcome, especially considering that her first attorney had tried to convince her to settle for just $15,000.

I think the key to our case was the credibility of the neurosurgeon. The defense couldn't find a neurosurgeon who would testify against him—he was just that good—and with his testimony we were able to put things into context for the arbitrator. We showed that he was very credible, and he said that the surgery was reasonable, appropriate, and necessary.

To be honest, Susan's first attorney was not completely wrong about her. She could be a challenging client. But she was being the "squeaky wheel" in advocating for herself and what she believed in. I had to convince her not to appeal the arbitrator's award, because juries' prejudices against premise liability plaintiffs posed some serious risks. One of the most serious risks was that, if we appealed the arbitrator's decision, but didn't improve the award by 30 percent ($100,000.00), she could potentially owe his attorney's fees because of the particular way Hawai'i court laws work. I could not bear the thought of this risk, because that would mean she could be victimized twice. I did not want this injustice for her. It would have been too much of a risk. Sometimes a client can do themselves more harm than good by appearing in front of a jury, and the attorney always has to take that into account. It can be a delicate negotiation.

One of the things that helped convince her not to appeal the award was that we were able to negotiate her medical bills with her insurance company. In a case like this, where the medical bills have initially been covered by the victim's health insurance, the insurance has to be paid back out of the eventual settlement. We were able to negotiate that payback down by a substantial amount, which meant that more of the award went back to Susan.

I was pleased that we were able to do so well for her; she had suffered a lot from the injury and deserved to be compensated for that. She deserved justice.

Chapter 6

Justice for Tina

EVERY PERSONAL INJURY CASE is about seeking justice for someone who has been harmed by the action or negligence of another person or entity. It's always a difficult situation for the person who has been harmed, and we are often moved by the stories our clients tell us. Tina, though, is a special case even among those stories. Her plight left all of us determined to leave no stone unturned in finding justice for her.

At the time of the accident, Tina was 88 years old. She lived at home with one of her daughters, but because of some kidney failure, she needed regular dialysis. Aside from the dialysis, she was in great health and spirit. She took care of all of the grandchildren, cooked for the family, and even walked to the market, a half hour trip each way, every day. Although she was living with family, there was no one who could take her to dialysis in the middle of the day three times a week. But, she qualified for a program that provided a kind of medical transport—similar to a handi-van—to pick her up at the house, take her to the dialysis clinic, and bring her back home. The service was contracted by the dialysis clinic. The transport driver has some simple medical training, and wheels the patient from their door into the van, and then from the van into the dialysis facility, whereas a regular handi-van usually just drops off the patient.

On this particular day, they came to pick Tina up as usual, she had her dialysis, and was on her way home. In fact, the van was trying to make a left turn into her street when the accident happened.

The transport van was hit by an oncoming pick-up truck as it was making the turn. It was a horrific accident. The van spun around and rolled over onto its side.

The intersection is governed by a stop sign. Supposedly, the truck had stopped and was proceeding forward from the stop sign as our transport driver was trying to make his left turn.

Whose fault was it? In this case both drivers had some fault. When you are making a left turn, you are supposed to yield to oncoming vehicles, whether they are coming toward you legally or illegally, so clearly the transport van driver was at least partly at fault. On the other hand, the impact was much too severe for the truck to have started from a complete stop at the stop sign. Either the truck driver stopped and then floored it, or never came to a complete stop at all. There is no way to tell for sure.

Tina passed out upon impact. Her wheelchair had been locked in place, but became dislodged with the force of the collision. She woke up with blood on her face, and thinking that it was hers, she felt around to see how she had been hurt. Although she used a wheelchair, she could walk a little bit, so she tried to get up, and was going to try to get out of the van. Tina may have been 88 years old, but she was tough. There was another wheelchair-bound patient in the van. Tina managed to dislodge herself from where she was, and reached over to the other patient, trying to wake him up so they could both exit the vehicle. He was dead. That was when she realized that the blood on her face was his, seeing that he was a bloody mess.

Tina wasn't bleeding from anywhere. She was severely injured, but all of her injuries were internal. So after trying to wake the other guy up and finding that he was dead or completely unresponsive, she tried to get out. That was when she realized that her leg and hip were broken. It turned out that her pelvis was also broken. She had managed to wiggle herself out of the wheelchair, but there was really nothing more she could do. So she waited and she passed out again. The next thing she remembers is the first responders breaking open the van with the jaws of life.

They took her out and put her in the ambulance. All she remembered was waking up a couple of times and then being at the hospital already.

At the hospital, Tina's family was very concerned. Tina kept saying that she wanted to go home, but she couldn't walk with the broken hip, pelvis and broken leg. The doctors insisted that she stay, but she kept pushing and pushing until they finally let her out early. She persuaded one of her grandchildren—they are all in their 40s, so they're not kids—to tell the hospital and the doctors that there would be somebody home to help her. That was not entirely true. They would take some time off to be with her, but she would not have somebody there 24/7, which was what she really needed.

Anyway, she got her way and went home. She couldn't get up the stairs, so they converted the living room into a makeshift bedroom for her, and she seemed to be doing fine. She wanted to resume her prior activities, and even managed to make it to the market and back, but she was really sore for the rest of the day. So she couldn't walk anymore after that. One of her children went to look at her leg and discovered that it was really black and swollen. It turned out that her pain was not from the walk, but from some gangrene that was developing in her leg. It was a vascular issue.

Ironically, the doctor said if she hadn't gone for that walk, they would not have known about the gangrene in her foot because they thought she was doing fine.

Tina had to go back to the hospital, and it turned out that there were a lot of vascular issues caused by her being so inactive while recovering from her injuries. She had been in the hospital for a couple of months, which meant she wasn't up and moving around, so she had developed necrosis. They removed some of it and gave her a lot of antibiotics. She was in the ICU for a couple of weeks. The doctors thought they had it under control, but it got worse and they ended up having to remove her big toe.

They let her go home, thinking the necrosis was under control, but they have had to remove more of the tissue from her foot. Tina had to go back to a rehab hospital so she could try to learn how to walk again. It turned out she was never able to go home again although she really yearned to go home, back to the life she loved.

Now she had these chunks of her foot actually missing. There was still an odor from the bacteria, but the doctors said that was the best they could do at the time.

Both of the vehicles in Tina's accident were company vehicles. The truck that hit her transport van was owned by a construction company; the passengers were all young, strong construction workers. They were not seriously hurt, except for one who was riding in the bed of the truck. He had to have back surgery. But this was obviously a high value case, with one person killed and the serious injuries suffered by Tina and the construction worker.

We filed a suit on Tina's behalf against both the truck driver and the construction company. I wanted to make sure that we could maximize the settlement to account for Tina's ongoing medical care, which looked like it might be permanent. But Tina said she just wanted to settle.

So we had a meeting at the rehab facility. Tina didn't speak much English—though I suspect she could speak and understand more than she admitted—so I brought my own translator because I wanted to be sure that she was not being pushed to do anything by any of her kids or grandkids. The translator was my former secretary, who is now retired, and I knew I could trust her completely. She had been with me for 20 years. There was a lot of money on the table, and I didn't want anyone else influencing Tina's decision.

Tina was as tough and spunky as always. We talked about the situation and I told her I thought I could get her a higher offer.

But she was determined. She said, "No. I want to settle now. I want this to be behind me. I don't care if I have to spend the rest of my life here in the hospital, but I don't want this lawsuit looming over me. Let's just get it done and settle it."

I said, "Okay, but before I let you go, I have to ask. Is there anybody who is forcing you or pushing you into this? Making you feel like you should settle instead of trying to hold out and get enough money so that we can pay your medical bills and everything?"

The look on her face was priceless. She just scoffed at me. All of the family members in the background started to giggle. It was clear that nobody bosses this woman around.

My translator was listening to them and laughing with them. She said, "Nobody tells Nana what to do, ever. Nana tells everybody else what to do."

So I said, "Okay," and we settled the case, even though the settlement was a little less than the value of the case.

It would not have been ethical for me to take less than value without asking her, and in a situation like this with an elderly person dependent on family, you worry that that are being manipulated for their money. I wanted to be sure that I was taking my direction from Tina and not from her family. I was able to walk away feeling very confident that it was her decision and no one else's. She had been through a lot and the quality of her life had been dramatically altered, but she wasn't in it for the money. She just wanted to put it all behind her and move on.

Ironically, even though we settled with the defendant's insurance company, we were still negotiating the underinsured motorist claim with Tina's own insurance company. Sometimes dealing with your own insurance can be even more difficult than dealing with the other side. It is a sad reminder that no matter how friendly they might appear at first, no insurance company is actually your friend.

Tina's justice was that she passed, knowing a settlement was in place, and that it would help take care of her family for years to come.

Chapter 7

Serving Clients in Many Ways

WHEN YOU ARE LOOKING for a lawyer for your personal injury case, the best advice I can offer is to find the one that is the right match for you. Every client is different, every law firm is different, and not every firm is a match for every client. As a client, you deserve to feel heard and valued by your lawyer—don't settle for less than that.

For many people, an auto accident or a slip-and-fall becomes their first-ever encounter with a lawyer. That can be a scary and stressful prospect, especially if all your ideas about lawyers come from TV or movies. On top of that, the client is often still dealing with the aftermath of serious injury, which adds its own pain and stress. As lawyers, we need to allay that stress, not add to it.

There's an old joke that says, "What do you call a thousand lawyers at the bottom of the sea? A good start." Lawyers have a reputation, deserved or not, for being scary and mean. It's a fact of life, and something that we have to take into account.

In my office, we are very conscious of the fact that visiting a lawyer for the first time can be an intimidating experience, and my team works hard to put those fears to rest. We're pretty down to earth, each in our different ways; I like to say that together we are "extra down to earth." People can feel very comfortable when they come here.

I think that comes from the fact that we are all local. We all grew up here in Hawai'i . None of us grew up with a lot of money, but we all grew up steeped in our Hawai'i an culture, and we are still plugged into that local culture.

George, for instance, is a paralegal from a place here in Honolulu called Waianae, which is known as a kind of tough neighborhood. He is able to relate really well with local people here. There is a Pidgin English that is commonly spoken here in Hawai'i , and George is much more fluent in Pidgin than I am. When I was young my grandmother would not let me speak Pidgin at all even though everyone else seemed to use it. In fact, several years ago Pidgin English became Hawai'i 's third official language. George is great at it, and is able to put local people at ease quickly when he starts talking.

Cindy, my assistant, is from an outer island. She relates to people really well. Jolie is my other paralegal. She and I are also local, but we don't sound as local as George and Cindy. I speak a more standard English, probably because I lived in the Midwest for eight years during college and law school. I think I picked up some of that flat Midwestern accent while I was there.

All of us work to put people at their ease. We realize how important it is to help new clients manage their fears and expectations. We take the time to listen to their story. We ask more questions and we dig deeper. That's also part of what makes us "extra down to earth." We take the extra time to ask more questions and get a bigger picture.

But we do find that new clients often get really nervous about meeting the attorney. It's especially common with clients who are immigrants. Earlier waves of immigrants are more ingrained into our culture, but the newer waves of immigrants come from places where you would probably never meet a lawyer. They might go to a doctor, but would never see a lawyer unless they were involved with a crime or something like that. So they get really nervous.

Sometimes a client will be chatting away with George and Jolie, but when I come into the room, they get quiet. I've had clients who break out into a sweat and don't want to say anything to me. We have to work at making them comfortable. Fortunately George is really good at that. He will crack a joke and get the ball rolling.

Many people hesitate to call a lawyer because they fear the expense. They are used to having to pay for legal services. When they need a criminal lawyer, or a divorce lawyer, or a contract lawyer, they know they will have to pay up front, and it can be extremely expensive.

But when someone has been injured in an accident, and maybe can't even work, how are they going to come up with money to hire a lawyer? The answer is, of course, that they are not.

What they often don't know is that personal injury lawyers work on a contingency basis. That means the client does not pay any fee up front. If there is no settlement or award, there is no charge.

We are always trying to educate people about the contingent basis of our work. I hate to see somebody lose out on a claim because they think they can't afford an attorney. If there is no claim made, the only entity that benefits is the insurance company. We all pay for insurance in case we made a mistake, and if you don't make a claim when you have one, then the insurance company profits even more.

The assistance we provide can go beyond the actual claim. We help our clients in many other ways as well.

We are sometimes called upon to help a client find a doctor. In Hawai'i , it can be hard to find a doctor who will take an automobile accident or a slip-and-fall case. That's because insurance companies have made it so time consuming to make a claim. Doctors are used to submitting their claim and being paid, but in a car accident case, they submit their claim, maybe wait 30 or 40 days for payment, and then on the 30th day, instead of payment they get more questions from the insurance company. The company wants clarification for this, or an apportionment issued for that, and the whole process takes too much time. Doctors sometimes have to hire staff specifically to deal with claims and handle records requests for personal injury clients, and many decide these cases are just not worth the effort. What is more, the doctors also must face their medical decisions being questioned by untrained insurance adjusters, something they clearly dislike.

Unlike Medicare and private health insurance, these no-fault companies will not just take the doctor's word for it that this person was injured and needed treatment. I find that doctors are sometimes offended by that, because they are not used to having their word or their opinion questioned.

That means it can be difficult for an accident victim to find a doctor who will treat their injuries. I know firsthand how difficult it can be to find a doctor after an accident. I had an accident myself years ago and even though I had been with my personal care provider for 20 years, they still denied me treatment. I called around and found that no one was taking car accident cases. I had to go to someone that I work with, simply because there was no one else.

Here in Hawai'i , we as lawyers are legally prevented from referring a patient to a doctor. Most lawyers believe as I do that the law is unconstitutional, but it is still on the books. Having done this work for so long, however, we do generally know which doctors will accept these patients, and we try to help our clients as much as we can. We are not allowed to make direct referrals, but we can and do recommend doctors. We often offer a client a few names to consider.

Helping our clients find treatment is just one of the ways that we extend our services. We maintain an ongoing relationship with our clients. We send birthday cards; we keep them in our family permanently. As part of that relationship, we have attended graduations, birthday parties, and weddings—all kinds of events. Some clients even keep in touch on Facebook.

Clients often call us for advice on other legal matters. It's understandable; ours is probably the only law office they know and they don't differentiate among legal specialties. I have to explain to them that I have little experience with things like wills and trusts, or divorce, so I am not the right person to advise them on such things. We always refer those clients out to attorneys that we trust.

We only do personal injury, but if you call us because you just don't know how to find a lawyer other than maybe the internet, we can definitely refer you to someone. And when we do make a referral, we take ownership for it. If the person we refer you to is not the right fit, we will try to help with that lawyer or find someone else for you.

We often get referrals from former clients. It's always nice when a client sends a friend or family member to us. Sometimes they even come to the appointment with the friend they are referring. The first time it happened, I was surprised, but the new client was an immigrant and I think they might have been intimidated coming to an attorney's office. So our client came with them for emotional support. We have since seen that happening with other clients as well.

In fact, one of my most memorable cases came about because a former client, who has become a good friend, asked me to take a look at it.

Bob had been injured in a moped accident, but his was not a typical personal injury case. He was having a hard time finding someone to take his case, and my former client, his aunt, called and asked me to see him. She told me it was a matter of justice because the police had beaten him up.

Bob's aunt is a social worker, and I guess you might call her a bleeding heart like me. As a favor to her I agreed to meet with Bob, and so she brought him in to see me. He seemed respectful and sincere—maybe because I was his last hope of getting representation—and he told us the story.

He was 17 at the time of the accident. He was riding along on his moped, and apparently must have done something—I don't know what—to draw the attention of a nearby cop. So the cop turned on his light and started chasing him. As often happens, when you do not comply immediately by stopping when cops are chasing you, they get very angry. The cop finally cornered Bob in an alley, where there were no other routes of escape. The cop banged Bob with his car, not horribly, but enough to knock him over. Then the cop got out of his car and started kicking and punching him.

That was how Bob came to be injured, not from his moped being pushed down. Fortunately for him, he was not badly hurt, but that weighed against him in finding representation. No one wanted to take on a case involving a police officer, especially where the injuries were not severe.

I had to at least consider the case because my client, Bob's aunt, had begged me to do it. And when I looked at it, it really did seem to be a case of excessive force. If Bob had been running away, I could maybe understand the cop tackling him, but he had already been knocked to the ground when the cop started beating on him. The department did not want to pay the claim, so we ended up having to file a lawsuit on Bob's behalf. In the course of discovery, I had to tailor-make the questions for the information I wanted.

One of the things I wanted was this cop's personnel file. The department fought me on it, but we went in front of the judge and the judge said I was entitled to it. They kept trying to delay delivering the file, even after the judge's ruling. Eventually their attorney called and told me they wanted to settle rather than turn over the file. I never did see the file, so I still don't know what was in it, but whatever was in there must have been bad. I suspect that there may have been statements in the internal incident report from officers who arrived on the scene and saw Bob getting beaten by their fellow officer.

I have been around cops all of my life. My dad was one for more than 25 years. I grew up calling all of his cop buddies "uncle." So, I knew firsthand how they close rank and stick up for each other out of sheer loyalty. I really respect that. So, if this one bad apple's police brothers weren't standing up for him, he really must have done wrong.

When the attorney called and said they wanted to settle, she asked me how much it would take. I gave her what I thought was a ridiculous number—you always ask for more than you think you can get—but she called back the next day and said it was done.

So we were able to do very well for Bob; he ended up getting much more than what someone with similar injuries might have received in a typical personal injury case. The truth is that I think he would have done well in front of a jury if it had gone that far, but I think his case is another good example of how our digging deeper and trying harder produces good outcomes for our clients.

In Conclusion

I WANT TO CONCLUDE by thanking you for reading this book. I hope you have found it enlightening, and if you know others who might benefit from reading it, please let me know and I will be happy to send them a copy.

I know there are people out there who have been injured or bullied in ways similar to the clients whose stories are included here. They may not know what to do. I believe they may benefit just from knowing that others have been there before them, and I want to show them that there is recourse for them. There are people willing to hear them out.

Personal injury firms like ours can walk you through an injury claim step by step. All you will need to worry about is going to the doctor and getting better. Worrying about your claim, and your insurance adjuster, and the law involved, and the statute of limitations, and all that kind of stuff, can bog you down and make your recovery even more difficult. Turning your case over to us means you can let all of that go and focus on getting better.

We stand up to bullies. We will stand up to anybody in town. There is no lawyer and no law firm in town that we are afraid of. Attorneys have tried to bully us, and we push right back just as hard as they push on us. I've had lawyers literally two inches from my face screaming and swearing at me, and I've pushed right back.

We've got your back and will always stand up for you.

Attorneys are taught never to represent themselves. Even though we know the law, our own case will be too personal. No one can be objective about their own case, and that may keep us from making the best decisions. The same goes for the public. Don't try to pursue a claim on your own.

I have had attorneys as clients, and when I had my accident, I had somebody else handle my case. There is a peace of mind to be found when you just leave it all up to the attorney to handle. Obviously you're going to make the decisions yourself with the attorney's guidance, but when you leave everything to the attorney, and you are free to recover from your injuries.

Personal injury cases can be a little more complicated than an average lay person would believe. Specific things need to be presented in specific ways, and if they are not presented properly, the value of your settlement can be greatly affected. There are precautions that you need to take to avoid having to repay liens or pay bills, and an attorney will negotiate those things for you.

Your attorney is always there when you speak to other lawyers or speak to insurance adjusters. We make sure that the adjusters or defense counsel don't take advantage of you by trying to get information that they're not entitled to—information that they can use against you or misconstrue. It is really important for people to have an attorney, especially in a personal injury claim.

If you are injured and want to preserve your rights, call an attorney. My philosophy in these cases is that you should call right away. I don't care how it looks. If you're calling your lawyer the next day after the accident or you're calling after you get home from the hospital, or whenever, some people may think that you're just in it for the money. That's not necessarily the case. You should call us right away, because there can be mistakes made all along the way that can have a dramatic effect on your case.

For instance, an insurance adjuster may call you when you're still lying in a hospital bed, or hopped up on Vicodin. They'll try to get information from you and you may misremember things because you're still so hurt and medicated. You may misspeak. These things can happen right away, so it's important that you have an attorney right away to watch out for you.

Lots of clients come to us after they've already talked to the adjuster, and the adjuster has—based on what the client said—already denied liability. That can be because it wasn't presented to them in the proper way, or because the adjuster asked leading questions that steered them into giving up their case. That does happen.

I know there is a lot of information online—there is information on our own website—but the law is fact-sensitive. Some of the laws that you see, or some of the things you read online are not going to apply to you, or might apply to you differently than you might think. That's why it's so important to have someone who is experienced in this area to help guide you through the process.

So call us and schedule a consultation. We'll be happy to help. At the Recovery Law Center, our promise to you is that we'll be in the recovery with you.

About the Author

For over 25 years, attorney Glenn Honda has helped people injured in accidents throughout Hawai'i get the best outcome for their case, whether it's maximizing their settlement, or balancing costs and risks vs. putting the whole experience behind them. As the founding attorney of the Recovery Law Center, he is passionate about helping his clients with their physical, emotional and financial recovery. Mr. Honda will fight to get you coverage for your medical bills, lost wages, damaged property and other costs related to your accident.

Professional Associations and Memberships

- Hawai'i State Bar Association, Member
- Hawai'i Association for Justice, Member
- American Trial Lawyers Association, Member
- National Academy of Personal Injury Attorneys
- Lawyers of Distinction
- The National Trial Lawyers, Top 100 Lawyers

Expert Press

www.ExpertPress.net

Made in the USA
Monee, IL
04 November 2026

67387325R10036